34421378R00063

Made in the USA
Lexington, KY
22 March 2019